Charge into Reading

Decodable Reader
with literacy activities

WORD ENDING

blends

The Bump
Word-Ending Blends

Brooke Vitale • Mila Uvarova

CHARGE MOMMY
BOOKS
Riverside, CT

Copyright © 2023 Charge Mommy Books, LLC. All rights reserved.

No part of this book may be reproduced or transmitted in any form or by any means, electronic or mechanical, including photocopying, recording, or by any information storage and retrieval system, without written permission from the publisher.

For information address contact@chargemommybooks.com
or visit chargemommybooks.com

Library of Congress Control Number: 2023904931

Printed in China
ISBN 978-1-955947-37-4
10 9 8 7 6

Designed by Lindsay Broderick
Created in consultation with literacy specialist Marisa Ware, MSEd

Flint pats a stump.
He and Brand want to jump on the stump.

GULP.
It is a big jump.

Flint must bend his legs to jump.
He bends.
He jumps!

"Is it a cramp?" Flint asks.
"It is a wasp!" Brand grunts.

Flint wants to help.
He helps Brand limp to the stump.

Brand spots a bump on his leg.
"It is the end!" Brand yelps.

Flint and Brand clasp hands.
Flint helps Brand stand.

Brand sulks as he limps past the pond.
Brand grunts as he limps up a ramp.

Brand yelps as he sits at the camp desk.

Brand spots his pals in the pond.
He wants to swim in the pond.

Brand jumps up.
He runs to the pond.

Flint gasps.
Brand!

Let's Talk Literacy!

Read the sentence below. Then circle the picture that matches the sentence.

Flint and Brand clasp hands.

Let's Talk Literacy!

Each of the words below contains a word-ending blend. Sound out each word. Then draw a line from **each word** to its **matching picture**.

  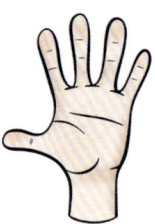

blimp   hand   milk   pond   stump   wolf

Let's Talk Literacy!

Say the name of each picture below. Then circle the words that contain a **word-ending blend**.

Answers: wolf, blimp, pump, hand

Let's Talk Literacy!

Read each word below. Then circle the pictures in each row that have names containing the same **word-ending blend**.

bump

bend

self

Answers: lamp, chimp, blimp / hand, sand, wand / elf, wolf

Let's Talk Literacy!

Say the name of each picture below. Then circle the correct **final consonant blend** for each word.

ld lk mp

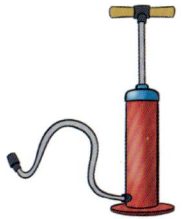

lk mp nt

ld mp nd

ld lk nd

lk mp nd

ld lk mp

Answers: milk, pump, lamp, pond, hump, stump

Let's Talk Literacy!

Write the letters that form each picture word in the boxes below. Then draw a **scoop mark** under each consonant blend.

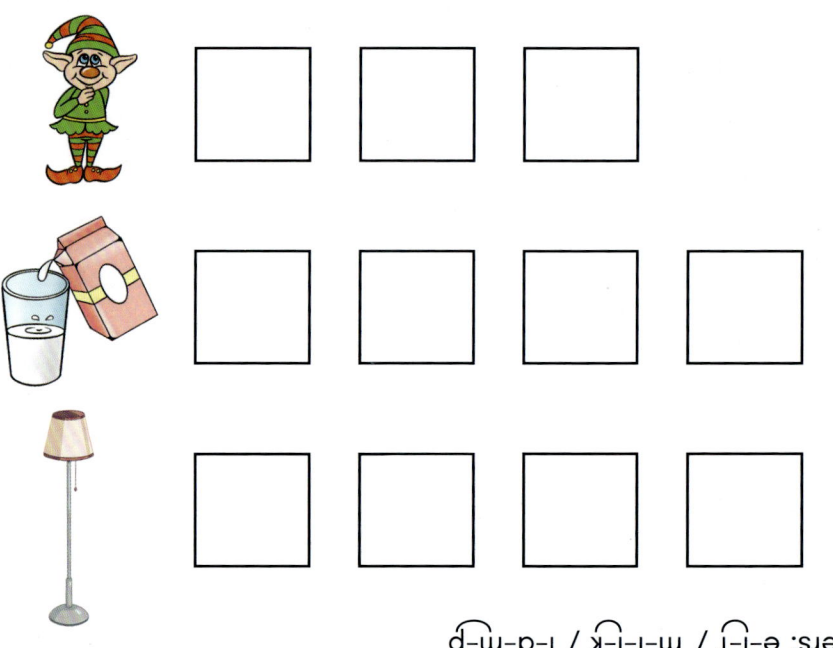

Answers: e-l-f / m-i-l-k / l-a-m-p

Let's Talk Literacy!

The name of each picture below ends with a different consonant blend. Sort the words in the **word bank** by putting them under the picture of the word that uses the **same consonant blend**.

| golf | limp | land | silk |
| elk | self | dump | bend |

  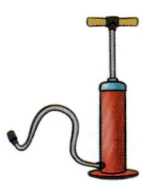 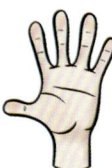

___ ___ ___ ___

___ ___ ___ ___

Let's Talk Literacy!

Say the name of each picture below. Then write the word's **final consonant blend** on the line below the picture. The first one has been done for you.

__nd_   _____   _____   _____

_____   _____   _____   _____

Answers: wand, milk, chimp, elf, pond, wolf, stump, hump